The Faces of Irish Civil War Soldiers

The Faces of Irish Civil War Soldiers

Compiled and Edited by

JoAnna McDonald

Rank and File Publications
1926 South Pacific Coast Highway Suite 228
Redondo Beach, California 90277
(310) 540.6601 Fax: (310) 540.1599
books@thirdwave.net

McDonald, JoAnna M., 1970 -

The Faces of Irish Civil War Soldiers / JoAnna McDonald 1st ed.
p. cm.
Includes bibliographical references.
ISBN: 1-888967-03-X

1. United States--History--Civil War, 1961--1863. Irish Soldiers.
2. Soldiers--Irish-American.
I. Title.

DA963.M34 1999 941.50922

Christmas Night '62

The wintry blast goes wailing by,
The snow is falling overhead;
I hear the lonely sentry's tread,
And distant watch-fires light the sky.

Dim forms go flitting through the gloom;
The soldiers cluster round the blaze
To talk of other Christmas days,
And softly speak of home and home.

My sabre swinging overhead
Gleams in the watch-fire's fitful glow,
While fiercely drives the blinding snow,
And memory leads me to the dead.

My thoughts go wandering to and fro,
Vibrating 'twixt the Now and Then;
I see the low-browed home again,
The old hall wreathed with mistletoe.

And sweetly from the far-off years
Comes borne the laughter faint and low,
The voices of the Long Ago!
My eyes are wet with tears.

I feel again the mother-kiss,
I see again the glad surprise
That lightened up the tranquil eyes
And brimmed thee o'er with tears of bliss,

As, rushing from the old hall-door,
She fondly clasped her wayward boy—
Her face all radiant with the joy
She felt to see him home once more.

My sabre swinging on the bough
Gleams in the watch-fire's fitful glow,
While fiercely drives the blinding snow
Aslant upon my saddened brow.

Those cherished faces all are gone!
Asleep within the quiet graves
Where lies the snow in drifting waves,—
And I am sitting here alone.

There's not a comrade here to-night
But knows that loved ones far away
On bended knees this night will pray:
"God bring our darling from the fight."

But there are none to wish me back,
For me no yearning prayers arise.
The lips are mute and closed eyes—
My home is in the bivouac.

William G. McCabe

Preface

Being a Celt by heritage and spirit I jumped at the chance to edit Faces of Irish Soldiers In the Civil War. Yet, before I could gather the photos of 200 Irishmen, I needed a criteria for these rough and ready individuals. Would they be pure bred Irishmen, men who were born in Ireland and moved to America, or first generation Irish-American? The challenge of research alone was extraordinary and overwhelming. The time involved in checking the family history of over 200 soldiers was simply unrealistic and thus abandoned.

On the other hand, if one is an avid student of Irish heritage, where would one look for a list of Irish surnames? As a product of the Internet generation, I connected to the web and typed "Irish Surnames." After surfing a bit I found it, names such as Callahan, O'Grady, Kelly, Cleary, McCarthy, Darley, and McDonald, of course, came up on the screen. In addition to the net, I found Michael O'Laughlin's book, The Complete Book For Tracing Your Irish Ancestors, very helpful. Therefore, with no disrespect intended, I essentially made a preliminary list of typical Irish names, names which still ring out on the green hills of Ireland.

I regret that some of the Irish who immigrated prior to the Civil War were a mix of several cultural groups and as such may not have considered themselves as "Irishmen." Their inclusion here is due solely to the ambiguity of their surnames. (My family, for example, is Irish, Scottish, Welsh, German, Italian, and we picked up Cherokee in Oklahoma and Arkansas —a fairly unique combination which makes us true Americans.)

Armed with my list I searched through hundreds of photographs at the Military History Institute in Carlisle, Pennsylvania, looking for interesting faces for your information and pleasure. It is my honor to present to you 200 photographs of Civil War soldiers with Celtic lineage.

Labor Day 1998
JoAnna Marie McDonald
Erin Go Braugh!

Introduction

When the call to arms went out in 1861 hundreds of Irishmen lined up at the recruiting stations. Unfortunately, there has never been a complete study of the actual number of Irish who fought in the Civil War. It would not, however, be unreasonable to state that thousands, if not hundreds of thousands, served in both the Confederate and Union armies— great names such as Patrick O'Rourke, Michael Corcoran, Thomas Meagher, David McIntosh, R.W. McGavock, Lloyd Tilghman fill many pages of our history books.

Unlike their English neighbors who, for the most part, assimilated into the Union and Confederate ranks, many Irishmen organized their own, unique units made up of their fellows and included the adjective "Irish" within their regimental names such as the 69th Pennsylvania Irish Regiment and the Irish Brigades of both the North and the South. Within these units one could find a wayward foreigner, but the majority carried the name of their Celtic ancestors.

The faces within represent the rank and file of the Irish legions, names which may not be readily known to the average student of the Civil War. Their families mourned as they disappeared into history leaving us their names, their songs and poems, their letters and battle accounts — and their photographs — to remind us of their passing and allow us to walk part of the way with them.

Herein are 200 photographs of those rugged Irish faces, some of whose portraits still hang on family walls or rest on fireplace mantels.

*****

Abbreviations:

Enl.= enlisted

Art.=Artillery

Cav.=Cavalry

Inf.= Infantry

Acknowledgments

As always I want to thank my family—Mom, Dad, sisters, nieces and nephews, the entire clan—and friends for their loyalty and encouragement. Les and Linda McDougall allowed me to borrow several books pertaining to Irish surnames. Nancy Baylor, assigned to the reference section of the Military History Institute, faxed me additional information on one of the soldiers.

The photographs herein were gleaned from the Military History Institute's rich photo archives. Michael J. Winey and Randy Hackenburg once again withstood my whirlwind visits; and though they assailed me with many good-natured jokes, they nevertheless stood ready to help whenever I needed assistance. As a matter of interest, the Institute is currently in search of any photographs of Civil War soldiers who served between 1861-1865. In addition, they welcome images pertaining to the United States Army or its personnel in any conflict.

Thanks as well go to the hundreds of individuals who have donated one or more photographs to the Military History Institute. Special mention includes: John Bigham, Curator of the South Carolina Confederate Relic Room (John provided me with information pertaining to several South Carolina boys); Clifford Breidinger of Trout Run, Pennsylvania; Martin Callahan of San Antonio, Texas who gave me permission to publish several of his photographs and sent me reference materials on the two soldiers; Martha A. Edwards, Cody, Wyoming mailed me information on her relative; Andrew German, Mystic, Connecticut, gave special permission for the use of his photographs; Bill Gladstone, Florida, provided one photograph; John Kuhl of Pittstown, New Jersey, graciously permitted me to use several of his images and sent additional information concerning these men; Joseph A. Matheson, Jr., Camden, South Carolina, provided additional material on one of the South Carolina boys and gladly gave his permission for the use of his photograph; Seward R. Osborne, Olivebridge, New York, allowed me to include one of his photographs, and Mrs. Albert Thornsberry, Sturgis, Kentucky, cordially replied to my letter concerning one of her relatives who is pictured in this book.

If you have a photograph of a Civil War soldier or a relative who fought in the Army at any time and would like to share your information with the Institute, please contact:

Michael Winey or Randy Hackenburg, Photo Curators
US Military History Institute
Carlisle Barracks
Carlisle, Pennsylvania 17013

Capt. A.B. Andrews
Co. B, 9th North Carolina Inf.
Enl. 1861, shot through the lungs, survived

Capt. W.H. Bagley
Co. A., 8th North Carolina Inf.
Captured 1862, paroled, transferred to 68th North Carolina, survived

Capt. G.P. Bailey, age 36
Co. K, North Carolina Inf.
Shot and stabbed in the Battle of Williamsburg May 1862, resigned in Oct. '62

2d Lt. Lucian R. Bailey, age 28
Co. F, 28th New York Inf.
Enl. 1861, wounded in 1862, discharged 1863

Faces of Irish Soldiers in the Civil War

Pvt. William R. Bailey
Co. A, 51st Georgia Inf.
Enl. 1862-1865 survived

Pvts. William T. and Henry M. Bailey
Co. C. 16th Georgia Inf.
William survived; Henry was captured in 1864, died in 1865

2d Lt. Joseph McRobert Baker
Capt. James Pickett's Independent Guard
Co. A, Florida Home Guard
Enl. 1861-1862, reenlisted in Co. I, 3d Georgia, discharged for disability 1863

Pvt. Absolom Barrett, age 22
Co. H, 51st New York Inf.
Enl. 1861, killed at Antietam, Sept. 17, 1862

Pvt. Alvin Barrett, age 24
Co. H, 5th New York Cav.
Enl. 1861, captured in '63, paroled and discharged 1864

Pvt. Charles M. Barrett
Co. I, 114th New York Inf.
Enl. 1862-1865, survived

Lt. Edward P. Barrett
Co. G, 50th Illinois Inf.
Enl. 1861-1862, resigned

1st Lt. George V. Barrett, age 24
Co. H, 23d Massachusetts Inf.
Enl. 1861-1864, survived

Faces of Irish Soldiers in the Civil War

Cpl. Michael Barrett, age 18
Co. I, 20th New York Cav.
Enl. 1863, mustered out 1865

Sgt. Maj. Nathan F. Barrett, age 18
156 New York Inf.
Enl. 1862, wounded in 1864, discharged 1865

Cpl. Samuel D. Barrett, age 25
Co. C, 51st Massachusetts Inf.
Enl. 1862, discharged 1863

1st Lt. Samuel E. Barrett
Battery B, 1st Regiment Illinois Art.
Enl. 1861-1864, survived

Pvt. John W. Bayley
Co. A, 3d Heavy Pennsylvania Art.
Enl. 1864-1865, survived

Pvt. Samuel B. Bearden
Co. B, 48th Alabama Inf.
Died of typhoid fever 1862

Capt. John H. Behan
Co. F, 16th West Virginia, USA
Enl. 1862, survived

Pvt. John A. Behrens
Co. A, 28th Pennsylvania Inf.
Enl. 1861-1865, survived

Faces of Irish Soldiers in the Civil War

Pvt. William B. Blair, age 26
Co. A, 9th Georgia Art.
Enl. 1864-1865, survived

Capt. Washington G. Bohaning, age 40
Co. D, 5th Arkansas Inf.
survived

Capt. Evans R. Brady
Co. K, 40th Pennsylvania (11th Reserves)
Enl. 1861, killed at South Mountain Sept. 14, 1862

1st Lt. George K. Brady
14th US Inf.
Regular Army officer, survived the war and remained in the US Army

Pvt. Edward A. Brandao
Fenner's Battery Louisiana Light Art.
Enl. 1862, in hospital '64, returned to duty, paroled '65

Pvt. Branson Breeden
Co. E, 10th Virginia Inf.
Enl. 1861, discharged 1862

Capt. George Brennan, age 25
Co. M, 14th New York Heavy Art.
Enl. 1863-1865, survived

2d Lt. E. K. Bryan
Co. I, 2d North Carolina Inf.
Enl. 1861, resigned and served as adjutant of the 31st North Carolina Inf.

Faces of Irish Soldiers in the Civil War

Pvt. Wesley Byrd, age 32
Co. B, Tennessee Art.
Enl. 1861, captured 1862, signed an oath of allegiance 1862

Pvt. Joseph P. Byers, age 26, Co. C, 18th Alabama Inf.
Enl. 1861-1862, deserted and joined the Union Army, Co. G, 1st Alabama Cav., USA, survived

Col. Richard Byrens, age 28
28th Massachusetts Inf.
Enl. 1862, wounded June 3, 1864 at Cold Harbor, died June 12, 1864

Pvt. Dennis Callahan
Co. I, 131st Pennsylvania Inf.
Enl. 1862, died Jan. 1863 from wounds received at Fredericksburg, Dec. 13, 1862

Cpl. George W. Callahan
Co. I, 138th Pennsylvania Inf.
Enl. 1862, transferred to Signal Corps, survived

Pvt. Richard Callahan
Co. B, 8th Pennsylvania Cav.
Enl. 1861, not accounted for on muster out roll

Pvt. John Maxwell Callaway
Battery B, 10th Battalion Virginia Heavy Art.
Surrendered with Lee at Appomattox

Pvt. William S. Callaway
Co. A, 9th Louisiana Inf.
Enl. 1861-1865, survived

Faces of Irish Soldiers in the Civil War

Sgt. Stephen H. Cannaday
Co. G, 21st Virginia Cav.
Enl. 1864-1865, survived

1st Lt. William W. Carmichael, age 18
Co. F, 52d North Carolina Inf.
Enl. 1862, captured April 2, 1865 paroled June 18, 1865

Maj. James Cavanaugh, age 34
69th New York Inf.
Enl. 1861, wounded at Fredericksburg Dec. 13, 1862, discharged 1863

1st Lt. Michael Clancy
Co. B, 5th New Jersey Inf.
Enl. 1862-1864, survived

Capt. Lewis Lee Clyburn, age 22
Co. G, 7th Battalion South Carolina Inf.
Enl. 1862, wounded in the leg, recovered and discharged May 1865

Pvt. Drury W. Coleman, age 36
Co. H, 2d Virginia Cav.
Enl. 1861, 1862 discharged

Capt. Alfred E. Colgan
Co. I, 28th Pennsylvania Inf.
Enl. 1861, wounded at Chancellorsville May 1863, discharged June 1864

Capt. Robert K. Collins
Co. I, 69th Indiana Inf.
Enl. 1862, discharged Jan. 1865

Pvt. Chifton Colvin
Co. B, 69th Pennsylvania Inf.
Enl. 1864-1865, survived

Cpl. Trustrim Connell
Co. I, 138th Pennsylvania Inf.
Enl. 1862-1865, survived

Pvt. Obediah G. Conner
Co. A, 25th North Carolina Inf.
Enl. 1861, deserted 1865

1st Lt. Henry M. Connolly
Co. C, 56th New York Inf.
Enl. 1861, discharged for disabilities 1862 survived

Sgt. B. Corbett and Capt. Edward P. Doherty
Co. L, 16th New York Cav.
Corbett, age 31, enl. '63, captured 1864, survived;
Doherty, age 24, enl. 1863-1865, survived

Father William Corby, with hat on knee
Irish Brigade, Army of the Potomac
survived

Capt. Jeremiah Coveney, age 24
Co. A, 28th Massachusetts Inf.
Enl. 1861, wounded May '64 at Spotsylvania, survived

Pvt. Patrick Coyle
Co. E, 69th New York Inf.
Enl. 1861, deserted 1863, No record on Phillip found

Faces of Irish Soldiers in the Civil War

Maj. St. Clair Dearing
25th North Carolina Inf.
Enl. 1861-1865, survived

Pvt. William G. Denham, age 28
Co. A, 1st Florida Inf.
Enl. June 1861, shot in the face Oct. '61, survived

Pvt. John G. Dromgoole, age 24
Co. G, 32d Texas Cav.
Enl. 1862, discharged 1865

Sgt. James E. Dunn, age 25
Co. K, 54th North Carolina Inf.
Enl. 1862-1865, survived

Pvt. James L. Dunnum, age 21
Co. D, 28th New York Inf.
Enl. 1861, wounded 1862, mustered out 1863

Quartermaster Sgt. Abner F. Durgin, age 21
2d New Hampshire Inf.
Enl. 1861-1865, survived

Lt. W. H. Egan
Co. E, 11th New Jersey
Enl. 1862, killed at Spotsylvania, May 12, 1864

1st Lt. Matthew W. Fatherly
Co. C, 56th North Carolina Inf.
Enl. 1861-1865, survived

Faces of Irish Soldiers in the Civil War

Col. Joseph Finegan, age 47
Provisional Army of the CSA from Florida
Enl. 1861-1865, survived

Col. Jesse J. Finley, age 49
6th Florida
Enl. 1862, severely wounded 1864, survived

Cpl. Edwin E. Finney
Co. E, 2d Wisconsin Inf. Ranked as a musician
Enl. 1861-1862 and Co. C, 46th Wisconsin 1865.
His brother fought for the Confederacy.

Pvt. William Fitzgerald
Co. E, 6th Virginia Cav.
Enl. 1862-1865, survived

Capt. James Fleming, age 19
Co. B, 28th Massachusetts Inf.
Enl. 1861, wounded three times in three separate engagements, survived

1st Lt. James G. Fleming, age 18
Co. C, 49th North Carolina Inf.
Enl. 1862, killed at Antietam, Sept. 17, 1862

Lt. Col. John A. Fleming
49th North Carolina Inf.
Enl. 1862, shot in the head and killed at the Battle of the Crater, July 1864

Sgt. Frank A. Fletcher, age 23
Co. G, 2d New Hampshire Inf.
Enl. 1861, wounded at Gettysburg, survived

Faces of Irish Soldiers in the Civil War

Sgt. John G. Floyd, age 20
Co. C, 11th North Carolina Inf.
Enl. Jan. 1862, captured in '64, survived

Pvt. Simon Fogarty
Co. F, 1st Regiment Charleston Guard
Enl. 1863, survived

Pvt. Matt M. Gaines
Co. E, 22d Alabama Inf.
Enl. 1862-1865, survived

Capt. James Gallagher, age 21
Co. E, 154th New York Inf.
Enl. 1862, wounded in action Dec. 1864, survived

Pvt. John Gallagher, age 40
Co. D, 38th Iowa
Enl. 1862-1865, survived

Col. Thomas F. Gallagher
40th Pennsylvania (11th Reserves)
Enl. 1861, wounded at South Mountain, Sept. '62, discharged Dec. 1862

Lt. Edward Geary
Battery E, Knap's Pennsylvania Independent Battery
Enl. 1861, wounded 1862, recovered, killed Oct. 29, 1863
at Wauhatchie, Tennessee

Sgt. Francis Gillam, age 22
Co. 11th North Carolina Inf.
Enl. Jan. 1862-Oct. '62, promoted to assistant surgeon

Faces of Irish Soldiers in the Civil War

Capt. J.M. Hadley
Asst. Surgeon, 4th North Carolina Inf.
Enl. 1862-1865, survived

1st Lt. William W. Higgins, age 45
Co. G, 1st South Carolina Rifles Inf.
Enl. 1861, survived

Cpl. Barrett S. Hunt, age 18
Co. K, 15th New York Engineers
Enl. 1864-1865, survived

Pvt. Oliver K. Irish, age 26
Co. A, 44th New York Inf.
Enl. 1861, killed at the Battle of Hanover Court House, May 1862

Pvt. Perry Irish
Co. B, 1st Regt. Vermont Vol. Heavy Art.
Enl. 1861-1865, survived

Capt. Robert Joyce
Co. F, 93d Ohio Inf.
Enl. 1862-1864, survived

1st Lt. H.C. Kearney
Co. E, 15th North Carolina Inf.
Enl. 1861, wounded four times in four different battles, captured in 1864, paroled in 1865

Maj. Philip Kearney
11th New Jersey Inf.
Enl. 1861, mortally wounded, July 2, 1863 at the Battle of Gettysburg, died August 1863

Faces of Irish Soldiers in the Civil War

1st Lt. Edward L. Kelley
Co. E, 9th Vermont Inf.
Enl. 1861-1865, survived

Capt. Moses Kelley
116th United States Colored Troops
survived

1st Lt. Charles Kelly, age 29
Co. I, 44th New York Inf.
Enl. 1862-1863, resigned

Sgt. Charles W. Kelly, age 26
11th Independent Battery New York Light Art.
Enl. 1861, wounded at Cold Harbor, 1864, discharged

Act. 3d Assistant Engineer Edward Kelly
United States Navy
Enl. 1865-1866, survived

Pvt. James Kelly, age 18
Co. L, 15th New York Cav.
Enl. 1864-1865, survived

1st Lt. James R. Kelly
Co. A, 1st Pennsylvania Cav.
Enl. 1861, wounded July 17, 1863 captured, survived

Pvt. Martin Kelly
Co. C, 100th Pennsylvania Inf.
Enl. 1864, not on muster out roll

Faces of Irish Soldiers in the Civil War

Capt. Michael Kelly
Co. G, 2d Connecticut Heavy Art.
Enl. 1862-1865, survived

Pvt. Michael Kelly
Co. K, 17th Pennsylvania Cav.
Enl. 1862, not on muster out roll

1st Lt. Robert Kelly, age 30
Co. D, 88th New York Inf.
Enl. 1861-1864, survived

Capt. S.A. Kelly, age 23
Co. G, 4th North Carolina Inf.
Enl. 1861, wounded at Chancellorsville
and Spotsylvania, captured at Winchester, 1864, survived

1st Lt. William B. Kelly, age 22
1st West Virginia, USA
Enl. 1861, detached from regiment Nov. 1861
to serve as a general's assistant

Capt. William F. Kelly, age 22
Co. G, 4th North Carolina Inf.
Enl. 1861-1863, resigned

Pvt. Abner McCharles Lay
Co. E, 13th Georgia Inf
Enl. 1861, captured at Spotsylvania, survived

Pvt. Samuel C. Lindsay, age 26
Co. G, 31st Virginia Inf.
Enl. 1861, survived

Pvt. Matthew R. Lindsey
Co. D, 29th Georgia Inf.
Enl. 1862, wounded in 1864, survived

Pvt. Sedley A. Lowd, age 20
Co. K, 2d New Hampshire Inf.
Enl. May 1861-1864, survived

Capt. Elkanah E. Lyon
Co. A, 44th North Carolina Inf.
Enl. 1862-1863, resigned

2d Lt. John B. Lyon
Co. C, 56th North Carolina Inf.
Enl. 1862, wounded and in hospital in 1865, paroled '65

2d Lt. John Lyon
Co. C, 7th South Carolina Inf.
Wounded in 1864, survived

Pvt. Henry H. Madden
Co. F, 99th Ohio Inf.
Enl. Aug. 1862, discharged 1863

Pvt. John H. Madden, age 21
Co. Unassigned, 21st New York Cav.
Enl. 1864-1865, survived

Capt. James Magner, age 28
Co. I, 28th Massachusetts Inf.
Enl. 1861, wounded at Gettysburg, July 3, 1863,
recovered but killed at Spotsylvania May 1864

Capt. Theodore Malloy
Co. E, 8th South Carolina Inf.
Enl. 1861-1865, survived

Pvt. James D. Malon, age 19
Co. G, 17th Mississippi Inf.
Enl. 1861-1865, survived

Sgt. George Manning, CSA
Co. G, 2d Maryland Inf.
Captured 1864, survived

Lt. Joseph R. Manson
Co. I, 12th Virginia Inf.
Enl. 1862, captured at Crampton's Gap, Sept. '62 released and survived

Capt. Samuel W. Maultsby
Co. H, 51st North Carolina Inf.
Wounded in the thigh May 1864, survived

Pvt. Anderson T. Mayo, age 20
Co. A, 26th Mississippi Inf.
Enl. 1861-1865, survived

Pvt. Robert D. Mayo, age 27
Co. I, 14th Georgia Inf.
Enl. 1861-1865, survived

1st Lt. Harvey C. McAllister, age 25
Co. H, 8th North Carolina Inf.
Enl. 1861, captured '62, released
rejoined the regiment, wounded at Petersburg, 1864, survived

1st Lt. Joseph A. McArthur
Co. I, 51st North Carolina Inf.
Enl. 1862, wounded in the chin, hip, right forearm and left arm at Drewry's Bluff, May 1864, survived

Sgt. Michael McCall
Co. C, 53d Pennsylvania Inf.
Enl. 1861, wounded at the Battle of Gettysburg, 1863, in the Wheatfield, survived

Capt. James McCallay
Co. B, 13th Georgia Inf.
Enl. 1861-resigned Aug. 1863

Pvt. Henry C. McCauley
Co. B, 1st Pennsylvania Inf.
Enl. 1861, wounded, survived

Capt. William H. McCauley
Co. C, 11th Tennessee Inf.
Enl. 1861-1865, survived

Sgt. James L. McClure
Co. G, 41st Pennsylvania (12th Reserves)
Enl. June 1861, wounded at Antietam, Sept. 17th, '62, died Oct. 9, '62

Pvt. Andrew M. McCord
Co. B, 11th Kentucky Cav.
Sept. '62, captured 1863, no further record

Pvt. David McCullough
Co. H, 116th Pennsylvania Inf.
Enl. 1861, wounded at Fredericksburg,
Dec. 13, '62, survived, transferred to Co. D, 116th PA

Pvt. Hezekiah McDaniel, age 20
Co. E, 45th Georgia Inf.
Enl. 1862, wounded three times, lost his left leg and sight in one eye, survived

1st Lt. Addams A. McDonald
Co. C, 45th Pennsylvania Inf.
Enl. 1861, wounded at Petersburg, 1864, survived

Pvt. Alexander S. McDonald
Co. K, 42d Pennsylvania Inf. "Bucktail"
Enl. 1861-transferred to the190th Pennsylvania Inf., May 1864, survived

2d Lt. Daniel M. McDonald
Co. B, 56th North Carolina Inf.
Enl. 1862, captured May 1863, took the oath of allegiance May 28, 1865

Capt. Hugh A. McDonald
Co. D, 1st Pennsylvania Cav.
Enl. 1861, wounded in 1862, court-martialed for distributing counterfeit money in 1864

Capt. James H. McDonald
Co. K, 50th New York Engineers
Enl. 1862-1863, survived

Pvt. Murdo McDonald, age 24
17th Independent Battery New York Art.
Enl. 1862-1865, survived

Sgt. Reid W. McDonald
Co. K, 22d Pennsylvania Cav.
Enl. 1864-1865, survived

Faces of Irish Soldiers in the Civil War

Pvt. Thomas McDonald, age 18
Co. K, 10th New York Heavy Art.
Enl. 1864-1865, survived

Pvt. William McDonald (left) and Sgt. Norton McDonald
Co. B, 29th Maine Inf. and 11th US Reg. Inf. resp.
enl. 1863-1865, survived

Pvt. William J. McDonald
Co. B, 56th North Carolina Inf.
Enl. 1863, wounded in the head May 1864, recovered

Pvt. Daniel McEachern, age 31
Co. I, 10th Georgia Inf.
Enl. May 1861, killed during Peninsula Campaign, June 1862

1st Lt. Hector McEachern
Co. D, 51st North Carolina
Enl. 1862, wounded in May 1864 in the right thigh and testicles, captured, survived and paroled 1864

Pvt. Pleasant Marion McEachern
Co. I, 10th Georgia Inf.
Enl. 1862-1865, survived

Capt. Robert J. McEachern
Co. D, 51st North Carolina Inf.
Enl. 1862, wounded at Cold Harbor
May 31, 1864, died of wounds June 1864

Pvt. David A. McElwain, age 18
Co. A, 2d Mississippi State Cav.
Enl. Dec. '62, captured May 1863, held at Fort Delaware, survived

Sgt. Maj. L.B. McFarland
Co. A, 9th Tennessee Inf.
Enl. 1861-1865, survived

Pvt. William G. McGahee
Co. G, 38th Georgia Inf.
Enl. 1862, deserted 1864

Pvt. William McGill, age 18
Co. C, 28th New York Inf.
Enl. 1861, killed at Cedar Mountain, Aug. 1862

Pvt. John McGraw
Co. M, 17th Pennsylvania Cav.
Enl. 1864-1865, survived

Pvt. Charles W. D. McHugh, age 22
Co. F, 24th Georgia Inf.
Enl. 1861, captured in '62, exchanged, survived

1st Lt. David G (standing) and Lt. Edward McIntosh
Co. B, "Pee Dee" Battery, South Carolina
Enl. 1861, both survived the war

Brig. Gen. James McIntosh, CSA
resigned from the US Army in 1861
joined the Confederacy and killed at Pea Ridge, March 7, 1862
His brother, John, fought for the Union

2d Lt. John B. McIntosh
2d US Cav.
Enl. 1861, served in several different outfits,
severely wounded in the leg in 1864, his leg was amputated,
survived. His brother James fought for the Confederacy

Capt. John C. McKenzie, age 26
Co. K, 10th Alabama Inf.
Enl. 1861, resigned Dec. '62
for medical reasons, reenlisted in Co. C, 53d Al., Cav., survived

1st Lt. E.T. McKethan
Co. K, 51st North Carolina Inf.
Enl. 1862, became sick but returned to his regiment, got sick again and furloughed Nov. 1864

Capt. David B. McKibbin
14th US Reg. Inf.
Accepted command of the 158th Pennsylvania, captured and died of disease. Chambers McKibbin was his brother.

2d Lt. Chambers McKibbin
14th US Reg. Inf.
Wounded three times during the war, survived

Pvt. Thomas McKie, age 16
Co. A, 11th Mississippi Inf.
Enl. 1862, mortally wounded July 3, 1863 in Pickett's Charge

Pvt. Solomon McLean, age 20
Co. D, 23d North Carolina Inf.
Enl. 1861, wounded at Malvern Hill 1862,
returned to duty in Oct. '62, wounded in '64, survived

Capt. Daniel McMahon, age 26
Co. D, 20th New York State Militia (80th NY Vol. Inf.)
Enl. 1861, wounded in '62 and in '63 at the Battle of Gettysburg,
his leg was amputated, and he was discharged 1864

Surg. Henry McMahon
11th Minnesota
Sept. 1864-June 1865, survived

Pvt. John McMahon (MacMahon), age 21
Co. B, 13th Massachusetts Inf.
Enl. 1861, wounded at Second Bull Run, taken prisoner at Gettysburg, survived

2d Lt. William H. McMahon, age 22
Co. K, 27th New York Inf.
Enl. 1861-1863, survived

Cpl. Michael McManus, age 23
Co. A, 2d New Hampshire Inf.
Enl. 1861, wounded at Gettysburg, survived, mustered out June 1864

Fife Maj. Alonzo J. McMaster
28th New York Inf.
In band, May 1861, discharged for disability Sept. 1861

Col. Fritz W. McMaster
17th South Carolina Inf.
Enl. 1861, captured in March '65, survived

Pvt. William McMinn
Co. H, 14th Mississippi Inf.
Enl. 1861-1865, survived

1st Lt. William McMurray
Co. B, 20th Tennessee Inf.
Wounded in the left arm during the siege of Atlanta, '64, his arm amputated, but he survived

Capt. J. F. McNeely, age 22
Co. K, 56th North Carolina Inf.
Enl. May 1862-1865, survived

Faces of Irish Soldiers in the Civil War

1st Lt. William R. McNeely, age 24
Co. A, 4th North Carolina Inf.
Enl. 1864, killed at Cedar Creek, Oct. 19, 1864

Surg. Daniel McRuer
2d Maine
Enl. 1861, promoted to brigade surgeon 1861, survived

Pvt. Joseph G. McWilliams
Co. H, 2d Virginia Inf.
Enl. 1861-1865, survived

Cpl. John Midgley, age 34
Co. B, 57th Massachusetts Inf.
Enl. Dec. 1863, wounded and captured May 1864, survived

Capt. Robert W. Mitchell
Co. B, 6th Pennsylvania Cav.
Enl. 1861-1864, survived

Pvt. Benjamin F. Mobley
Co. A, 22d Mississippi Inf.
Enl. 1861, wounded 1864, survived

Pvt. Elias Murphy
Co. I, 16th Louisiana Inf.
Enl. 1861, discharged 1862

Pvt. John Murphy, age 19
Co. K, 87th New York Inf.
Enl. 1861, wounded 1862, transferred and survived

Faces of Irish Soldiers in the Civil War

Capt. William F. Murphy
Co. K, 51st North Carolina Inf.
Enl. 1862, served throughout the war and was paroled 1865

Pvt. William S. Murphy
Co. D, 28th Pennsylvania Inf.
Enl. 1861, wounded at Gettysburg, July 3, 1863, discharged

Capt. William H. Murray, CSA
at Gettysburg he commanded Co. A, 1st Maryland Battalion,
Enl. 1861, killed July 3, 1863, Culp's Hill, Gettysburg

Pvt. Henry H. Nethery
Co. I, 38th Virginia Inf.
Enl. June 1861, received medical discharge in Dec. 1861

Sgt. Robert T. Nethery, age 40
Co. I, 8th North Carolina Inf.
Enl. 1861, captured at Cold Harbor 1864, died in prison Oct. 1864

Pvt. John P. Nicholson
Co. K, 28th Pennsylvania Inf.
Enl. 1861, promoted to commissary sergeant, survived

Capt. Garrett Nowlen
Co. G, 116th Pennsylvania Inf.
Enl. 1862, wounded at Fredericksburg Dec. 13, '62, recovered and transferred to Co. D, 116th PA, killed in 1864

Sgt. James H. Nugent
Co. G, 28th Pennsylvania Inf.
Enl. 1861, wounded in 1864, survived

Faces of Irish Soldiers in the Civil War

Pvt. Patrick Henry O'Connor
Allegheny Light Art. Virginia
Enl. 1862, transferred to Carpenter's Art. Unit, captured 1864, survived

Sgt. T. O'Doane
Co. B, 11th New Jersey Inf.
Enl. 1862, wounded in the head at Gettysburg, transferred to Veteran Reserve Corps, survived

Col. Patrick O'Rorke
140th New York Inf.
Graduated from West Point 1861, commissioned in the engineers and served as a staff officer until 1862, took command of the 140th in the fall of '62, killed on Little Round Top, July 2, '63 while leading his regiment

Sgt. Amos Olney
Battery A, 1st Rhode Island Light Art.
Enl. 1861-1865, survived

Pvt. Robert P. Owen
Co. B, 17th Alabama Inf,
Killed at the Battle of Franklin, 1864

Rev. George Patterson
Chaplain of the 3d North Carolina Inf.
Enl. 1863-1864, survived

Pvt. William V. Pauley (postwar)
Co. G, 2d Arkansas Cav.
Enl. 1861-1865, survived

Capt. Samuel J. Ridley
Co. A, 1st Mississippi Light Art.
Enl. 1861, killed at the Battle of Champion's Hill, May '63,
awarded the Confederate Medal of Honor, posthumously

Faces of Irish Soldiers in the Civil War

Pvt. William R. Ridley, age 19
Co. G, 6th Virginia Inf.
Enl. 1861, killed at 2d Manassas, Aug. '62

Lt. Col. James Rion
7th Battalion South Carolina Inf.
Enl. 1861, wounded twice near Petersburg 1864, survived

Cpl. John G. Ryan
Co. B, 12th Mississippi Cav.
Enl. 1862-1865, survived

Capt. John P. Sellman, age 21
Co. K, 1st Virginia Cav.
Enl. 1861, transferred to Co. A, 1st Maryland Cav., CSA, survived

Pvt. Tillman Shealy
Co. F, 51st Alabama Cav.
Absent Nov. and Dec. 1863, returned and captured June 1863, died Sept. 1863 as a prisoner of war

Sgt. Robert J. Southerland, age 19
Co. A, 43d North Carolina Inf.
Enl. 1862, wounded and captured at Gettysburg, paroled 1865

Capt. Jeremiah Sullivan (on right)
Co. I, 2d Michigan Cav.
Enl. 1863-1865, survived

2d Lt. Nimrod K. Sullivan
Co. C, 1st South Carolina Orrs Rifles Inf.
Captured July 14, 1863, released June 1865

Faces of Irish Soldiers in the Civil War

Pvt. William S. Sullivan
Co. H, 4th Kentucky Cav.
Enl. Sept. 1862, no further record

Pvt. Sanford F. Tippery
Co. C, 53d Pennsylvania Inf.
1862, not on muster-out roll

Pvt. Eliphalet N. Walsh, age 33
Co. E, 7th New York Heavy Art.
Enl. 1863, captured in June 1864, died of disease Aug. 1864

Pvt. Thomas P. Walsh
Co. A, 29th Pennsylvania Inf.
Enl. 1864-1865, survived

JoAnna McDonald

Photo Credits

USAMHI: United States Military History Institute Photo Archives, Carlisle, Pennsylvania, Curators Michael J. Winey and Randy Hackenburg.

Histories: Walter Clark, Histories of the Several Regiments and Battalions from North Carolina in the Great War 1861-1865, 1901.

Second New Hampshire: Martin Hayes, A History of the Second Regiment New Hampshire Volunteer Infantry in the War of the Rebellion, 1896.

Capt. A.B. Andrews, Histories
Capt. W.H. Bagley, Histories
Capt. G.P. Bailey, Histories
2d Lt. Lucian R. Bailey, USAMHI
Pvt. William R. Bailey, Mrs. Connie E. Fields via USAMHI
Pvts. William T. and Henry M. Bailey, Georgia State Archives via USAMHI
2d Lt. Joseph McRobert Baker, Lt.Col. Jessie McGraw via USAMHI
Pvt. Absolom Barrett, USAMHI
Pvt. Alvin Barrett, USAMHI
Pvt. Charles M. Barrett, USAMHI
Lt. Edward P. Barrett, Richard K. Tibbals via USAMHI
1st Lt. George V. Barrett, USAMHI
Cpl. Michael Barrett, USAMHI
Sgt. Maj. Nathan F. Barrett, Bill Gladstone via USAMHI
Cpl. Samuel D. Barrett, USAMHI
1st Lt. Samuel E. Barrett, USAMHI
Pvt. John W. Bayley, USAMHI
Pvt. Samuel B. Bearden, Mrs. Grace Thorton via USAMHI
Capt. John H. Behan, USAMHI
Pvt. John A. Behrens, USAMHI
Pvt. William B. Blair, Larry O. Blair via USAMHI
Capt. Washington G. Bohaning, Fay Bohaning via USAMHI
Capt. Evans R. Brady, USAMHI
1st Lt. George K. Brady, USAMHI
Pvt. Edward A. Brandao, Sandra Todaro via USAMHI
Pvt. Branson Breeden, Carole Foutz via USAMHI
Capt. George Brennan, USAMHI
2d Lt. E.K. Bryan, Histories
Pvt. Wesley Byrd, Kenneth Byrd via USAMHI
Pvt. Joseph P. Byers, Norma Y. Garbert via USAMHI
Col. Richard Byrens, USAMHI
Pvt. Dennis Callahan, Peggy Myers via USAMHI
Cpl. George W. Callahan, via USAMHI
Pvt. Richard Callahan, USAMHI
Pvt. John M. Callaway, Mrs. Albert Thornsberry via USAMHI
Pvt. William S. Callaway, J.E. Callaway via USAMHI
Sgt. Stephen H. Cannaday, Mrs. Anita C. Adkins via USAMHI
1st Lt. William W. Carmichael via Histories
Maj. James Cavanaugh, USAMHI
1st Lt. Michael Clancy, John Kuhl via USAMHI
Capt. Lewis L. Clyburn, Joseph A. Matheson via USAMHI
Pvt. Drury W. Coleman, Mrs. Hazel Lee Coleman Martin via USAMHI
Capt. Alfred E. Colgan, Ron Beifuss via USAMHI
Capt. Robert K. Collins, Frank Josek via USAMHI
Pvt. Chifton Colvin, USAMHI
Cpl. Trustrim Connell, Russ Pritchard via USAMHI
Pvt. Obediah G. Conner, Mrs. JoAnn Shepherd via USAMHI
1st Lt. Henry M. Connolly, USAMHI
Sgt. B Corbett and Capt. Edward Doherty, William Adams via USAMHI
Father William Corby, USAMHI
Capt. Jeremiah Coveney, USAMHI
Pvt. Patrick Coyle, USAMHI
Maj. St. Clair Dearing, Majorie J. Stone via USAMHI
Pvt. William Denham, Florida State Archives via USAMHI
Pvt. John G. Dromgoole, Martin Callahan
Sgt. James E. Dunn, Mrs. Edna L. Prather via USAMHI
Pvt. James L. Dunnum, USAMHI
Quarter-Master Sgt. Abner F. Durgin, 2d New Hampshire
Lt. W.H. Egan, Sergeant Thomas Marbaker, History of the Eleventh New Jersey Volunteers, 1898
1st Lt. Matthew W. Fatherly, Histories
Col. Joseph Finegan, Library of Congress via USAMHI
Col. Jesse J. Finley, Library of Congress via USAMHI
Cpl. Edwin E. Finney, Doris Finney Liebrecht via USAMHI
Pvt. William Fitzgerald, Nancye J. Page via USAMHI
Capt. James Fleming, Dr. Kathleen Dietrich via USAMHI
1st Lt. James G. Fleming, Histories
Lt. Col. John A. Fleming, Histories
Sgt. Frank A. Fletcher, 2d New Hampshire
Sgt. John G. Floyd, Histories
Pvt. Simon Fogarty, Lt. Col. John F. Reynolds via USAMHI
Pvt. Matt M. Gaines, Mrs. Neoma O. O'Brien via USAMHI
Capt. James Gallagher, USAMHI
Pvt. John Gallagher, Margaret Strouts via USAMHI
Col. Thomas F. Gallagher, Roger Hunt via USAMHI
Lt. Edward Geary, USAMHI
Sgt. Francis Gillam, Histories
Capt. J. M. Hadley, North Carolina State Archives via USAMHI
1st Lt. William Higgins, South Carolina Library via USAMHI
Cpl. Barrett S. Hunt, USAMHI
Pvt. Oliver K. Irish, USAMHI
Pvt. Perry Irish, USAMHI
Capt. Robert Joyce, USAMHI
1st Lt. H.C. Kearney, Histories
Maj. Philip Kearney, USAMHI
1st Lt. Edward L. Kelley, USAMHI
Capt. Moses Kelley, USAMHI
1st Lt. Charles Kelly, USAMHI
Sgt. Charles W. Kelly, USAMHI
Act. 3d Assistant Engineer Edward Kelly, USAMHI
Pvt. James Kelly, USAMHI
1st Lt. James R. Kelly, Andrew German via USAMHI
Pvt. Martin Kelly, USAMHI
Capt. Michael Kelly, USAMHI
Pvt. Michael Kelly, USAMHI
1st Lt. Robert Kelly, Kathleen Dietrich via USAMHI
Capt. S.A. Kelly, Histories
1st Lt. William B. Kelly, Gil Barrett via USAMHI
Capt. William F. Kelly, USAMHI
Pvt. Abner McCharles Lay, Merrill Smith via USAMHI
Pvt. Samuel C. Lindsay, Ashcraft Coll. via USAMHI
Pvt. Matthew R. Lindsey, Ms. Pearl Flowers via USAMHI
Pvt. Sedley A. Lowd, 2d New Hampshire
Capt. Elkanah E. Lyon, Histories
2d Lt. John B. Lyon, Histories
2d Lt. John Lyon, John Lyon Bradley via USAMHI
Pvt. Henry H. Madden, Ms. Sherry Patterson via USAMHI
Pvt. John H. Madden, Michael Aikey via USAMHI
Capt. James Magner, USAMHI
Capt. Theodore Malloy, Augustus Dickert, History of Kershaw's Brigade with Complete Roll of Companies, 1899
Pvt. James D. Malon, Ruth Shipp Yarbrough via USAMHI
Sgt. George Manning, Gil Barrett via USAMHI
Lt. Joseph R. Manson, William T. Zielinski via USAMHI
Capt. Samuel W. Maultsby, Histories
Pvt. Anderson T. Mayo, Toy A. Mayo via USAMHI
Pvt. Robert D. Mayo, Toy A. Mayo via USAMHI
1st Lt. Harvey C. McAllister, Histories
1st Lt. Joseph A. McArthur, Histories
Sgt. Michael McCall, Irvin Myers Coll.
Capt. James McCallay, Mrs. Claudin Dollar via USAMHI
Pvt. Henry C. McCauley, Mrs. Martha A. Edwards via Gettysburg National Military Park
Capt. William H. McCauley, Regimental Histories of the Tennessee Regiments
Pvt. James L. McClure, USAMHI
Pvt. Andrew M. McCord, John W. McCord, jr. via USAMHI
Pvt. David McCullough, Joseph Kelly via USAMHI
Pvt. Hezekiah McDaniel, Brenda Sorensen via USAMHI
1st Lt. Addams A. McDonald, Roger Hunt via USAMHI

Photo Credits (Cont'd.)

Pvt. Alexander S. McDonald, Mrs. Edward Falk via Harrisburg Round Table via USAMHI
2d Lt. Daniel M. McDonald, Histories
Capt. Hugh A. McDonald, Andrew German via USAMHI
Capt. James H. McDonald, USAMHI
Pvt. Murdo McDonald, USAMHI
Sgt. Reid W. McDonald, Frederich Weiser via USAMHI
Pvt. Thomas McDonald, USAMHI
Pvt. William McDonald and Sgt. Norton, Beverly H. Kallgren via USAMHI
Pvt. William J. McDonald, Histories
Pvt. Daniel McEachern, Beth Kissel via USAMHI
1st Lt. Hector McEachern, Histories
Pvt. Pleasant Marion McEachern, Beth Kissel via USAMHI
Capt. Robert J. McEachern, Histories
Pvt. David A. McElwain, Mr. Martin Callahan via USAMHI
Sgt. Maj. L. B. McFarland, Regimental Histories of the Tennessee Regiments
Pvt. William G. McGahee, Melba Smith via USAMHI
Pvt. William McGill, USAMHI
Pvt. John McGraw, USAMHI
Pvt. Charles W.D. McHugh, Mr. Russell J. Otters via USAMHI
1st Lt. David and Lt. Edward McIntosh, Joseph McIntosh via USAMHI
Brig. Gen. James McIntosh, Millers, Photographic History of the Civil War
2d Lt. John B. McIntosh, John Kuhl via USAMHI
Capt. John C. McKenzie, William O. Grimes via USAMHI
1st Lt. E.T. McKethan, Histories
Capt. David B. McKibbin, USAMHI
2d Lt. Chambers McKibbin, USAMHI
Pvt. Thomas McKie, Maud M. Brown, The University Greys: Company A Eleventh Mississippi Regiment, 1940
Pvt. Solomon McLean, R. Carol McLean via USAMHI
Capt. Daniel McMahon, Seward R. Osborne, jr. via USAMHI
Surg. Henry McMahon, Firelands Historical Society, Norwalk, Ohio, via USAMHI
Pvt. John McMahon, Scott Hahn via USAMHI
2d Lt. William H. McMahon, USAMHI
Cpl. Michael McManus, 2d New Hampshire
Fife Maj. Alonzo J. McMaster, USAMHI
Col. Fritz W. McMaster, Fitzhugh McMaster via USAMHI
Pvt. William McMinn, B.J. Martha Deal via USAMHI
1st Lt. William McMurray, Regimental Histories of the Tennessee Regiments
Capt. J. F. McNeely, Histories
1st Lt. William R. McNeely, Histories
Surg. Daniel McRuer, James Vickery via James Mundy via USAMHI
Pvt. Joseph G. McWilliams, Leoneita C. Milner via USAMHI
Cpl. John Midgley, Mike Mancuso via USAMHI
Capt. Robert W. Mitchell, Alex Chamberlain via USAMHI
Pvt. Benjamin F. Mobley, Mrs. Lula Whitworth via USAMHI
Pvt. Elias Murphy, Mrs. Pat Nickel via USAMHI
Pvt. John Murphy, Craig Nannos via USAMHI
Capt. William F. Murphy, Histories
Pvt. William S. Murphy, Ron Beifuss via USAMHI
Capt. William H. Murray, McHenry Howard, Recollections of a Confederate Staff Officer, 1914
Pvt. Henry H. Nethery, Marshall Neathery via USAMHI
Sgt. Robert T. Nethery, Marshall Neathery via USAMHI
Pvt. John P. Nicholson, USAMHI
Capt. Garrett Nowlen, USAMHI
Sgt. James H. Nugent, Cliff Breidinger via USAMHI
Pvt. Patrick Henry O'Connor, Grady A. O'Connor via USAMHI
Sgt. T. O'Doane, History of the Eleventh New Jersey Volunteers, 1898
Col. Patrick O'Rorke, USAMHI
Sgt. Amos Olney, Thomas Aldrich, The History of Battery A, First Rhode Island Light Artillery, 1904
Pvt. Robert P. Owen, Mrs. Robert Kerr via USAMHI
Rev. George Patterson, Histories
Pvt. William V. Pauley, A.C. Williams via USAMHI
Capt. Samuel J. Ridley, David Harris via USAMHI
Pvt. William R. Ridley, K. Mark Katz via USAMHI
Lt. Col. James Rion, Lt. Col. James A. Gabel via USAMHI
Capt. John G. Ryan, D. Mark Katz via USAMHI
Capt. John P. Sellman, Charles T. Jacobs via USAMHI
Pvt. Tillman Shealy, Jeff Shealy via USAMHI
Sgt. Robert J. Southerland, Histories
Capt. Jeremiah Sullivan, Mrs. Ellen Van Nieuwenhayzen via USAMHI
2d Lt. Nimrod K. Sullivan, South Carolina Library via USAMHI
Pvt. William S. Sullivan, George Lindsey via USAMHI
Pvt. Sanford F. Tippery, Norman Plank via USAMHI
Pvt. Eliphalet N. Walsh, USAMHI
Pvt. Thomas P. Walsh, USAMHI

en Van Nieuwenhayzen via USAMHI
2d Lt. Nimrod K. Sullivan, South Carolina Library via USAMHI
Pvt. William S. Sullivan, George Lindsey via USAMHI
Pvt. Sanford F. Tippery, Norman Plank via USAMHI
Pvt. Eliphalet N. Walsh, USAMHI
Pvt. Thomas P. Walsh Louis Hill, Poems and Songs of the Civil War (Gramercy Books: New York)

Index